THE BRAIN

Activity:
1. Find a coloring sample on the book covers.
2. Color the picture below and Fill in the Labelling.
3. Can you tell the major functions of the Brain?
4. How can you take care of your Brain?

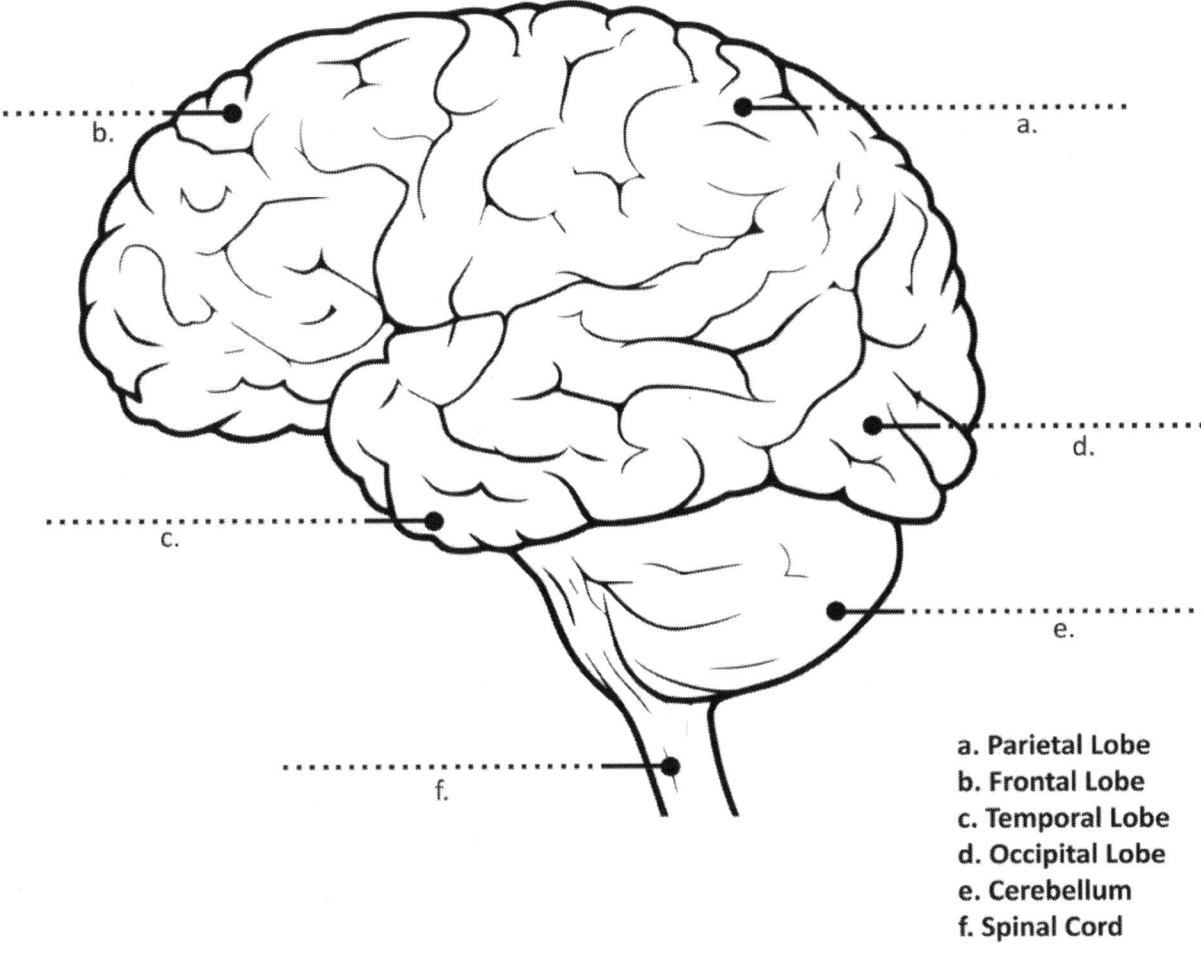

a. Parietal Lobe
b. Frontal Lobe
c. Temporal Lobe
d. Occipital Lobe
e. Cerebellum
f. Spinal Cord

Major Functions of the Brain:
The brain performs functions like interpreting touch, vision and hearing, as well as speech, reasoning, emotions, learning, and fine control of movement.

How you can care for your Brain:
Eat healthy foods, engage in mental exercises such as puzzle or Math problems, engage in physical exercises, avoid smoking and alcohol abuse.

THE HEART

Activity:
1. Find a coloring sample on the book covers.
2. Color the picture below and Fill in the Labelling.
3. Can you tell the major functions of the Heart?
4. How can you take care of your Heart?

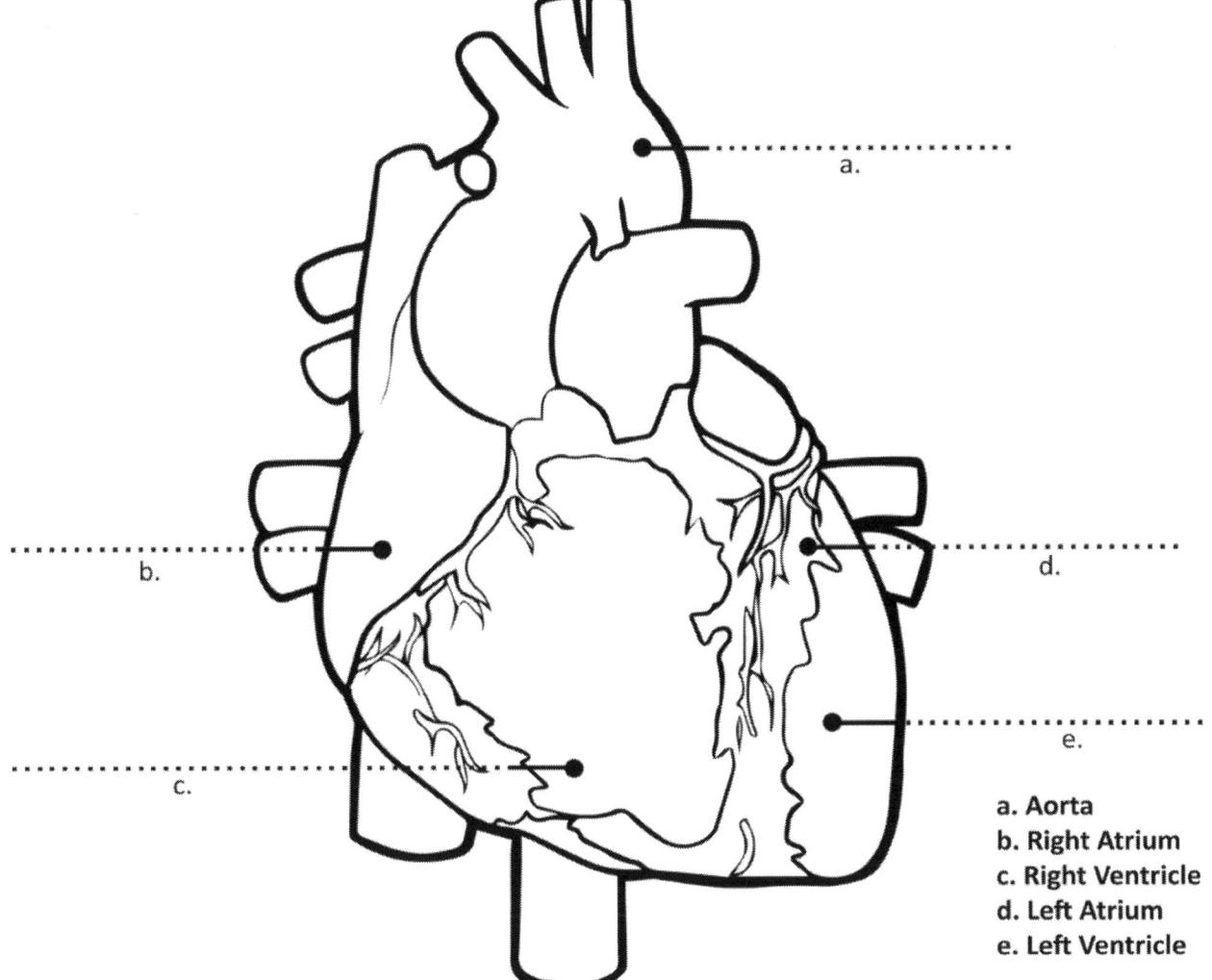

a. Aorta
b. Right Atrium
c. Right Ventricle
d. Left Atrium
e. Left Ventricle

Major Functions of the Heart:
The heart pumps blood throughout the body via the circulatory system, supplying oxygen and nutrients to the tissues and removing carbon dioxide and other wastes.

How you can care for your Heart:
Exercise regularly, Get enough sleep, Eat blanced diet and avoid smoking.

THE EYE

Activity:
1. Find a coloring sample on the book covers.
2. Color the picture below and Fill in the Labelling.
3. Can you tell the major functions of the Eye?
4. How can you take care of your Eye?

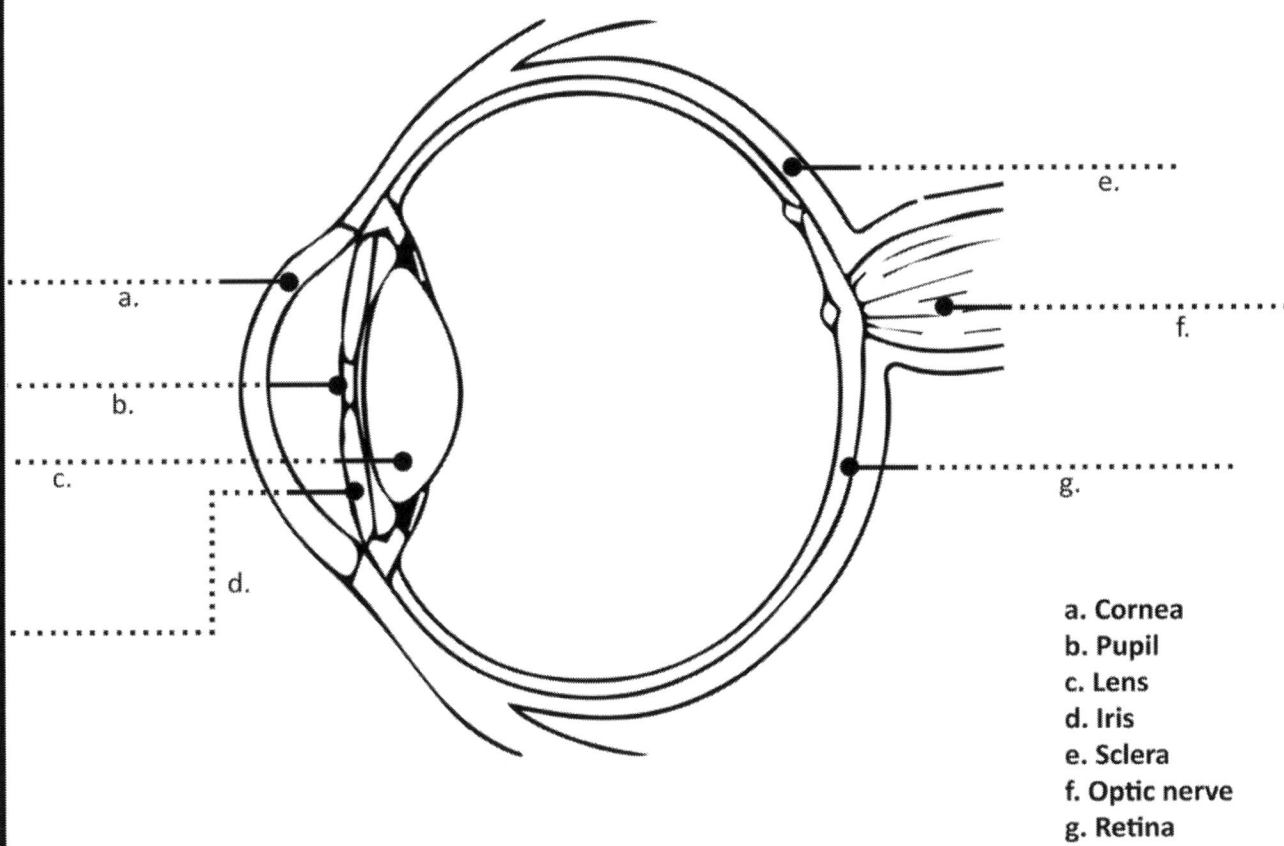

a. Cornea
b. Pupil
c. Lens
d. Iris
e. Sclera
f. Optic nerve
g. Retina

Major Functions of the Eye:
The Eye is the body's camera. In addition to giving you vision, your eye also provides depth perception and contributes to your balance.

How you can care for your Eye:
Eat a healthy, balanced diet, Get regular exercise, Wear sunglasses, Avoid smoking, Take regular breaks while doing computer work, Visit Your Eye Doctor Regularly.

THE PELVIC GIRDLE

Activity:
1. Find a coloring sample on the book covers.
2. Color the picture below and Fill in the Labelling.
3. Can you tell the major functions of the Pelvic girdle?
4. How can you take care of your Pelvic girdle?

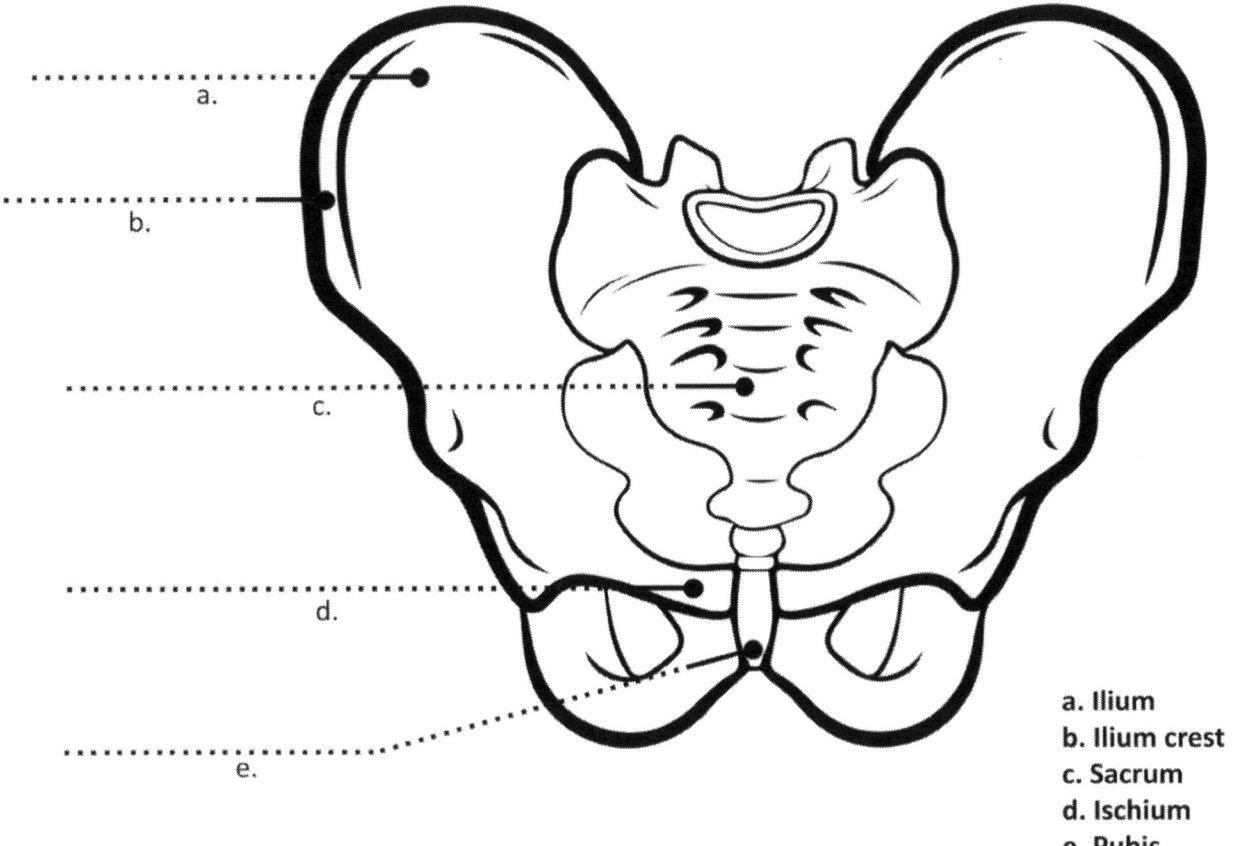

a. Ilium
b. Ilium crest
c. Sacrum
d. Ischium
e. Pubis

Major Functions of the Pelvic girdle:

Connects the trunk and the legs, supports and balances the trunk, and contains and supports the intestines, the urinary bladder, and the internal sex organs.

How you can care for your Pelvic girdle:

Get enough vitamin D to keep your bones strong, Vitamin D helps you absorb calcium in foods. You can find vitamin D in: Milk, Margarine, Egg yolks, Fatty fish like salmon and sardines.

THE MALE REPRODUCTIVE SYSTEM

Activity:
1. Find a coloring sample on the book covers.
2. Color the picture below and Fill in the Labelling.
3. Can you tell the major functions of the Male Reproductive System?
4. How can one take care of the Male Reproductive System?

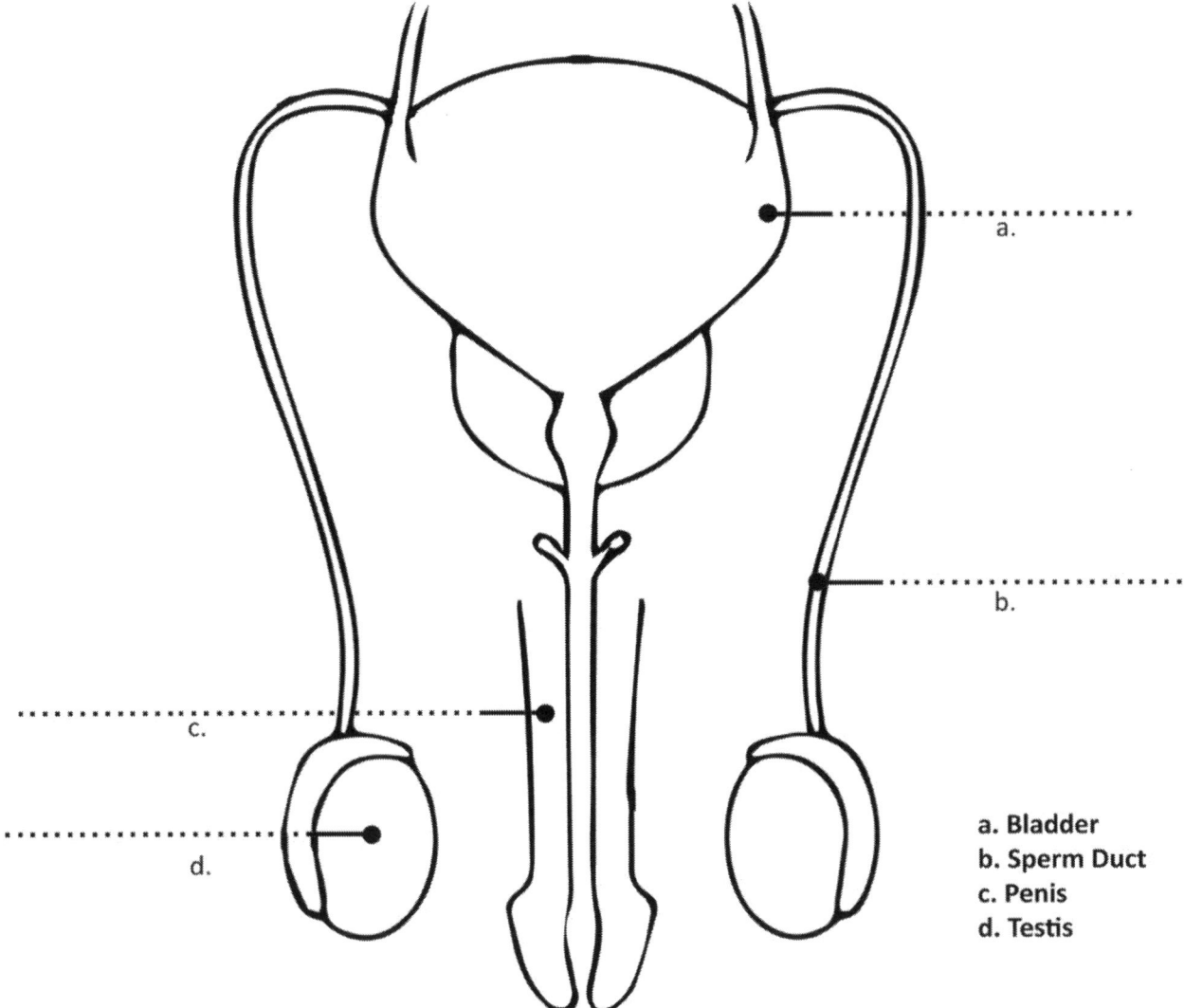

a. Bladder
b. Sperm Duct
c. Penis
d. Testis

Major Functions of the Male Reproductive System:
The production of male sex hormones, the formation of sperm, and the placement of sperm in the female reproductive tract, where one sperm can unite with a female sex cell.

How one can care for the Male Reproductive System:
Self exams, Protection from trauma, cleanliness, and medical checkups.

THE FEMALE REPRODUCTIVE SYSTEM

Activity:
1. Find a coloring sample on the book covers.
2. Color the picture below and Fill in the Labelling.
3. Can you tell the major functions of the Female Reproductive System?
4. How can one take care of the Female Reproductive System?

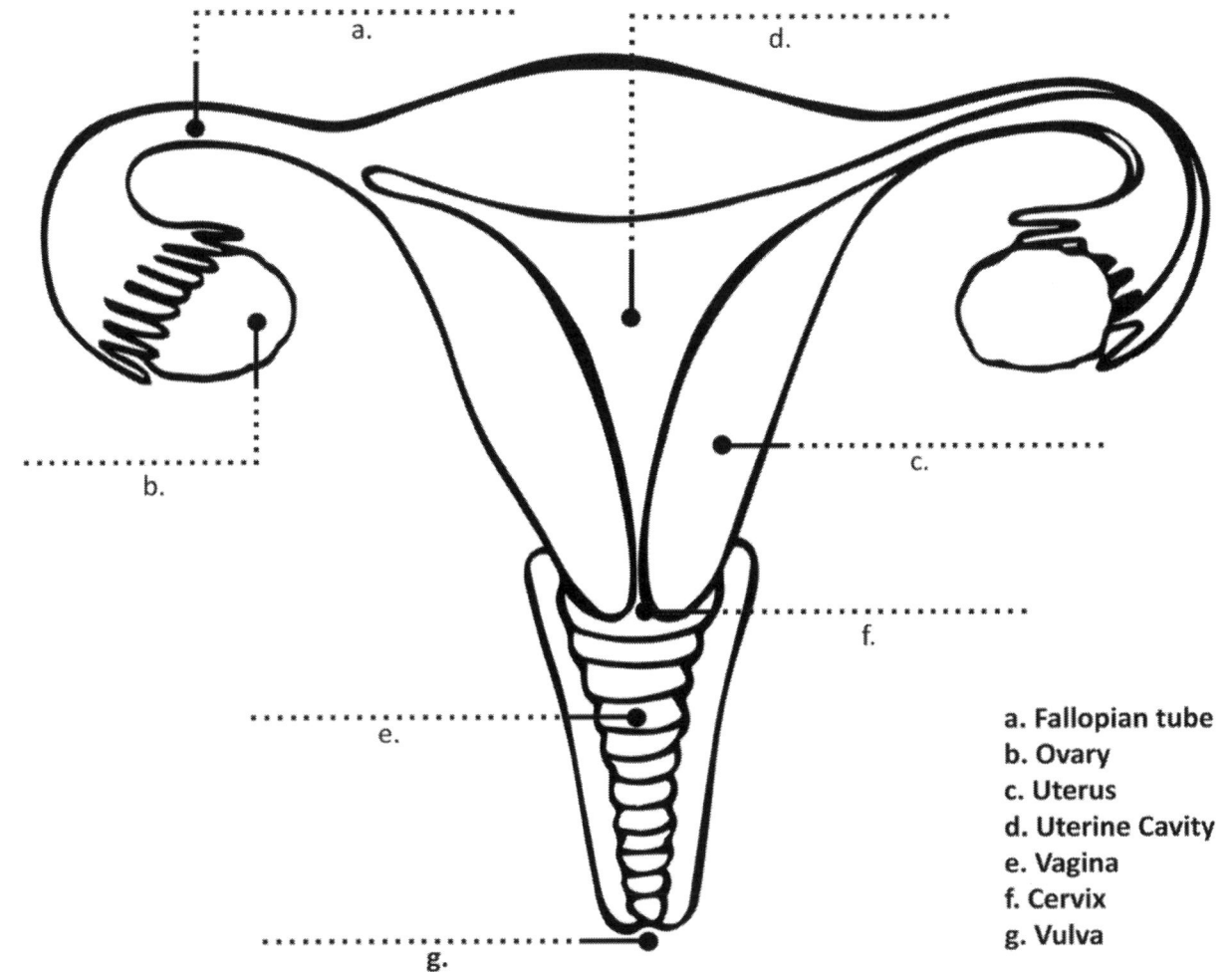

a. Fallopian tube
b. Ovary
c. Uterus
d. Uterine Cavity
e. Vagina
f. Cervix
g. Vulva

Major Functions of the Female Reproductive System:
It produces the female egg cells necessary for reproduction, called the ova or oocytes.

How one can care for the Female Reproductive System:
Drink a lot of water, self-exams, Cleanliness, medical checkups.

THE ARM

Activity:
1. Find a coloring sample on the book covers.
2. Color the picture below and Fill in the Labelling.
3. Can you tell the major functions of the Arm?
4. How can you take care of your Arm?

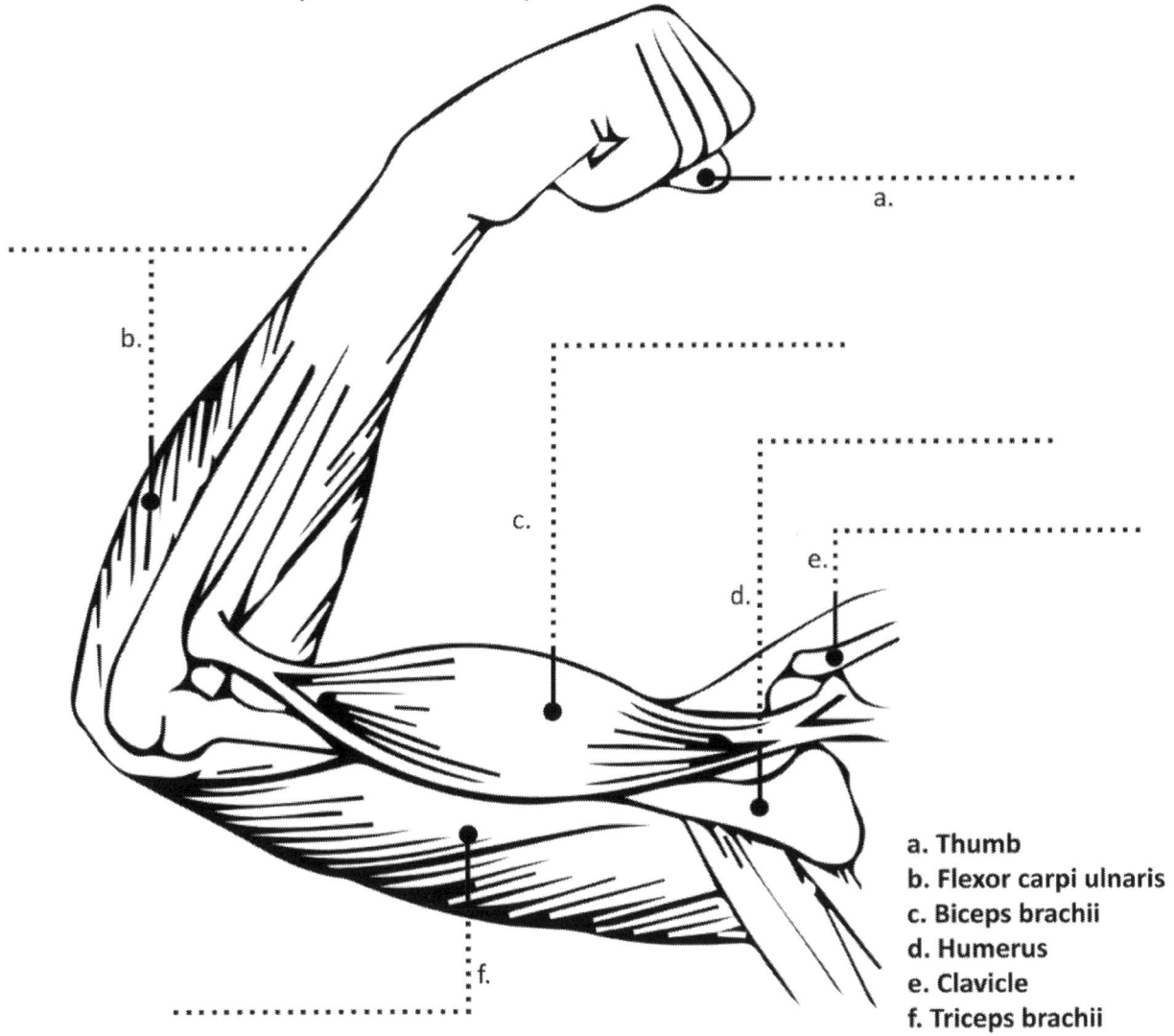

a. Thumb
b. Flexor carpi ulnaris
c. Biceps brachii
d. Humerus
e. Clavicle
f. Triceps brachii

Major Functions of the Arm:
The arm is used to reach out and grab anything, from food to tools to hand-holds, that may be helpful.

How you can care for your Arm:
Engage in stretching exercises (such as Yoga) as they will help to improve the flexibility of your arm

THE CELL

Activity:
1. Find a coloring sample on the book covers.
2. Color the picture below and Fill in the Labelling.
3. Can you tell the major functions of the Cell?
4. How can you take care of your Cell?

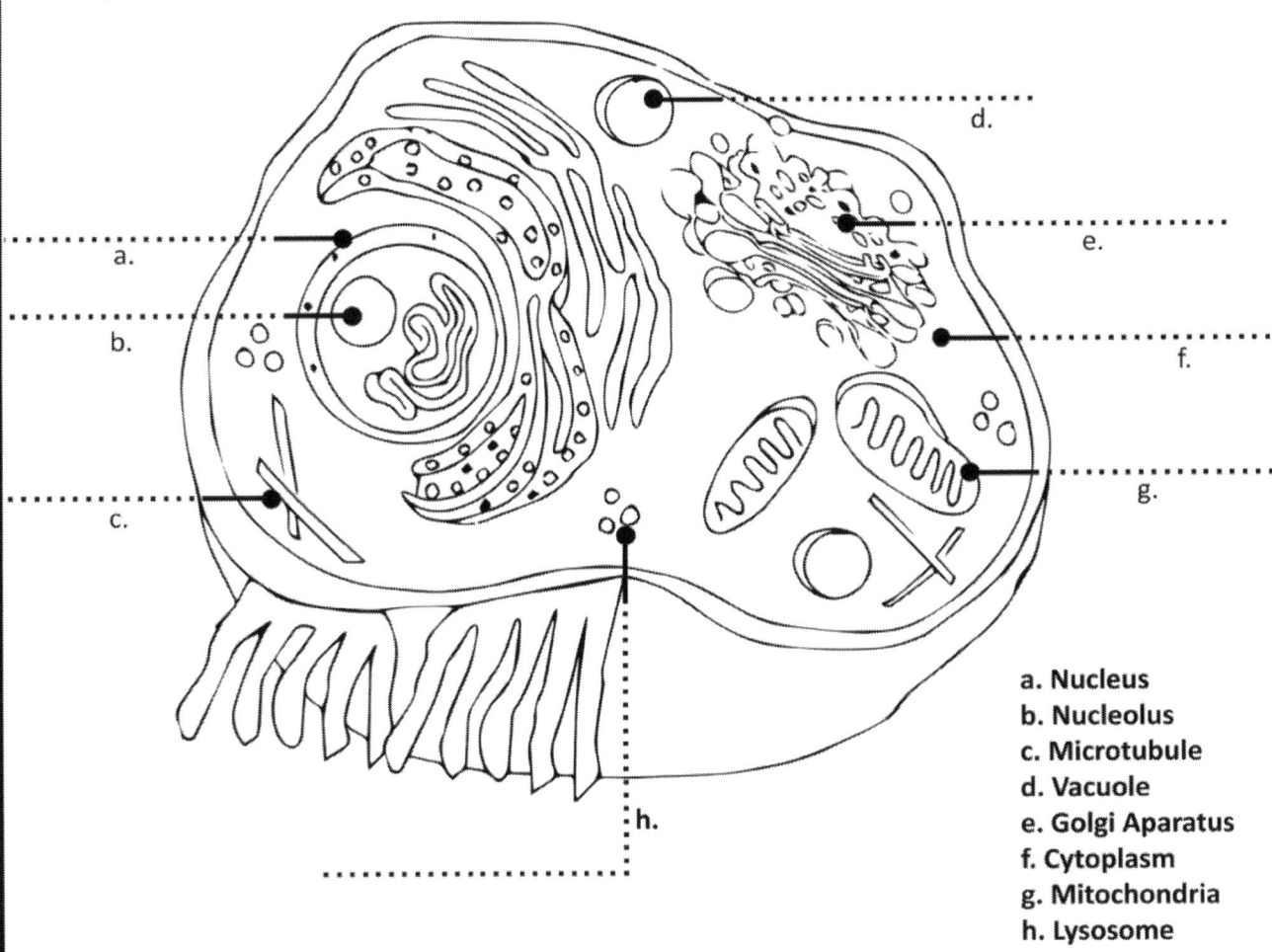

a. Nucleus
b. Nucleolus
c. Microtubule
d. Vacuole
e. Golgi Aparatus
f. Cytoplasm
g. Mitochondria
h. Lysosome

Major Functions of the Cell:
Cells take in nutrients from food, convert those nutrients into energy, Cells also contain the body's hereditary material and can make copies of themselves.

How you can care for your Cell:
Nourish your cells by eating pure, whole, natural, fresh foods like fruits and vegetables.

THE FEMALE BREAST

Activity:
1. Find a coloring sample on the book covers.
2. Color the picture below and Fill in the Labelling.
3. Can you tell the major functions of the female Breast?
4. How can one take care of the Breast?

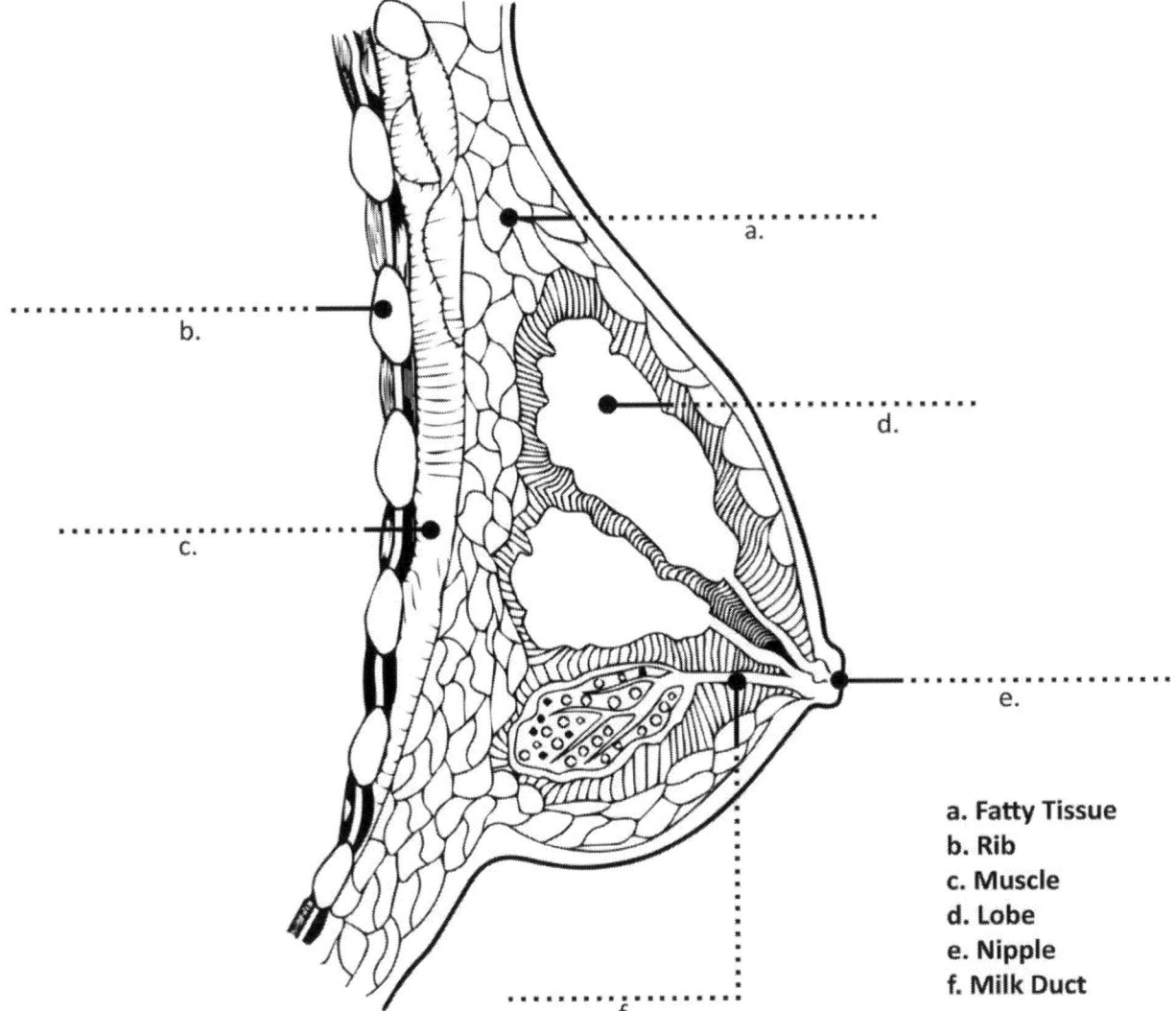

a. Fatty Tissue
b. Rib
c. Muscle
d. Lobe
e. Nipple
f. Milk Duct

Major Functions of the Breast:
The major function of the female breast is to produce milk in order to nourish an infant, a process called lactation.

How one can care for the Breast:
Eat a healthy diet, avoid smoking, avoid alcohol abuse, avoid harsh soaps, engage in regular exercises.

THE EAR

Activity:
1. Find a coloring sample on the book covers.
2. Color the picture below and Fill in the Labelling.
3. Can you tell the major functions of the Ear?
4. How can you take care of your Ear?

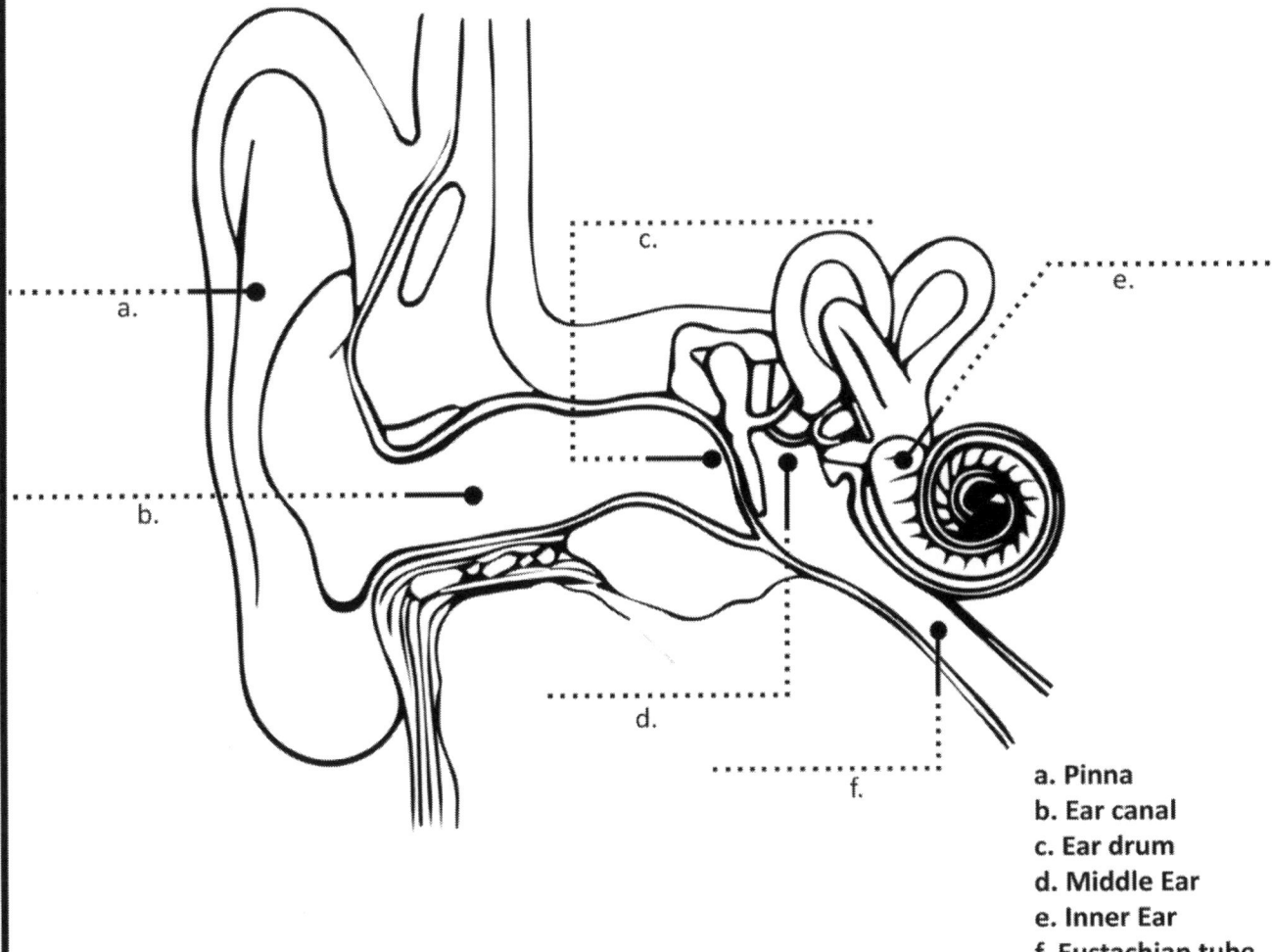

a. Pinna
b. Ear canal
c. Ear drum
d. Middle Ear
e. Inner Ear
f. Eustachian tube

Major Functions of the Ear:
The ear has two main functions; hearing and balance. It helps to detect, transmit and transduce sound, and also helps to maintain our sense of balance.

How you can care for your Ear:
Use earplugs around loud noises, Take medications only as directed, Keep your ears dry, Remove ear wax properly (don't use a cotton swab — they can push wax even deeper).

THE SKIN

Activity:
1. Find a coloring sample on the book covers.
2. Color the picture below and Fill in the Labelling.
3. Can you tell the major functions of the Skin?
4. How can you take care of your Skin?

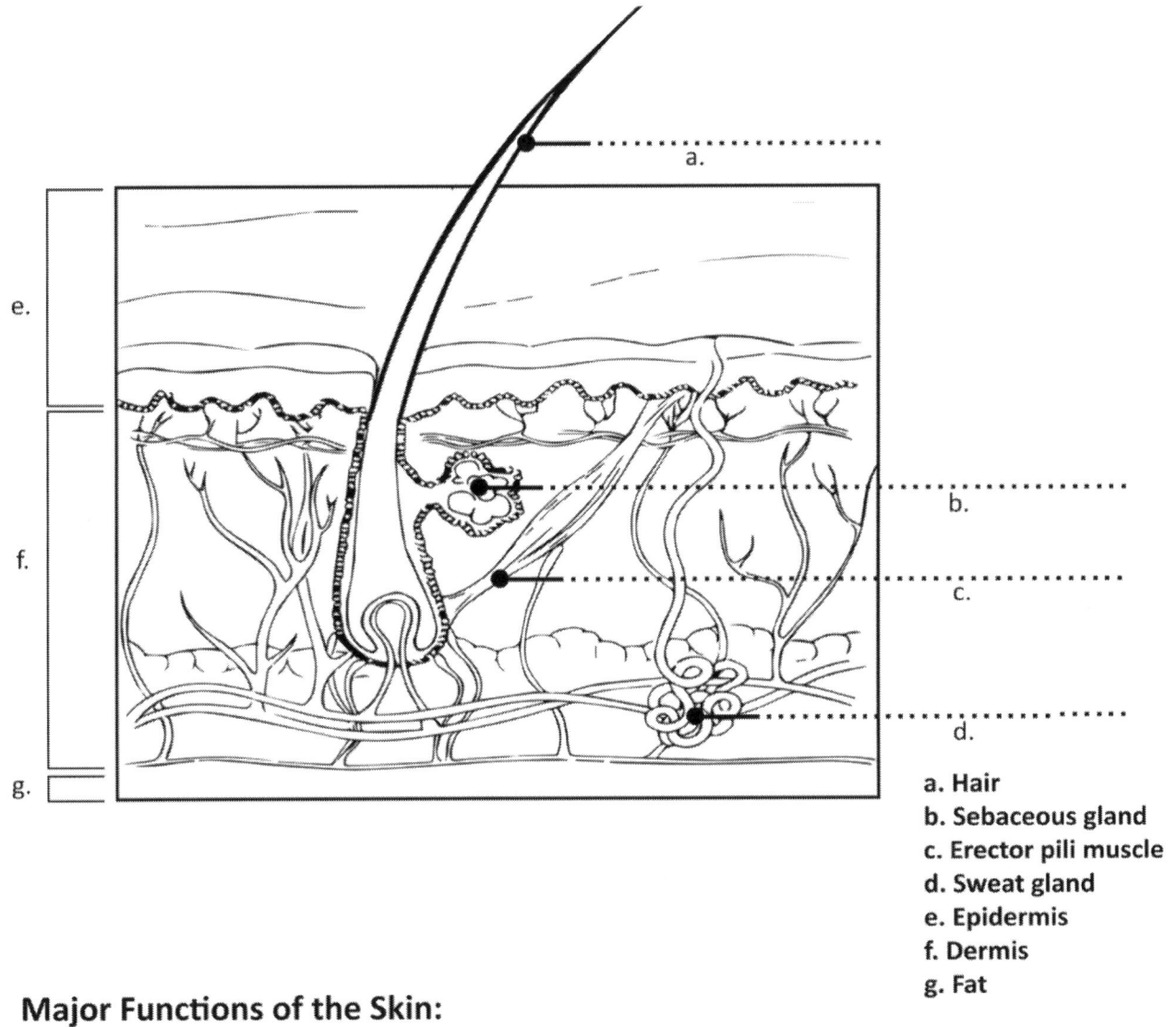

a. Hair
b. Sebaceous gland
c. Erector pili muscle
d. Sweat gland
e. Epidermis
f. Dermis
g. Fat

Major Functions of the Skin:
The skin has three main functions: protection (against toxins, radiation and harmful pollutants), regulation (body temperature) and sensation (a sensory organ to detect touch and temperature).

How you can care for your Skin:
Protect yourself from the sun, Daily cleansing, avoid smoking, Eat a healthy diet.

THE STOMACH

Activity:
1. Find a coloring sample on the book covers.
2. Color the picture below and Fill in the Labelling.
3. Can you tell the major functions of the Stomach?
4. How can you take care of your Stomach?

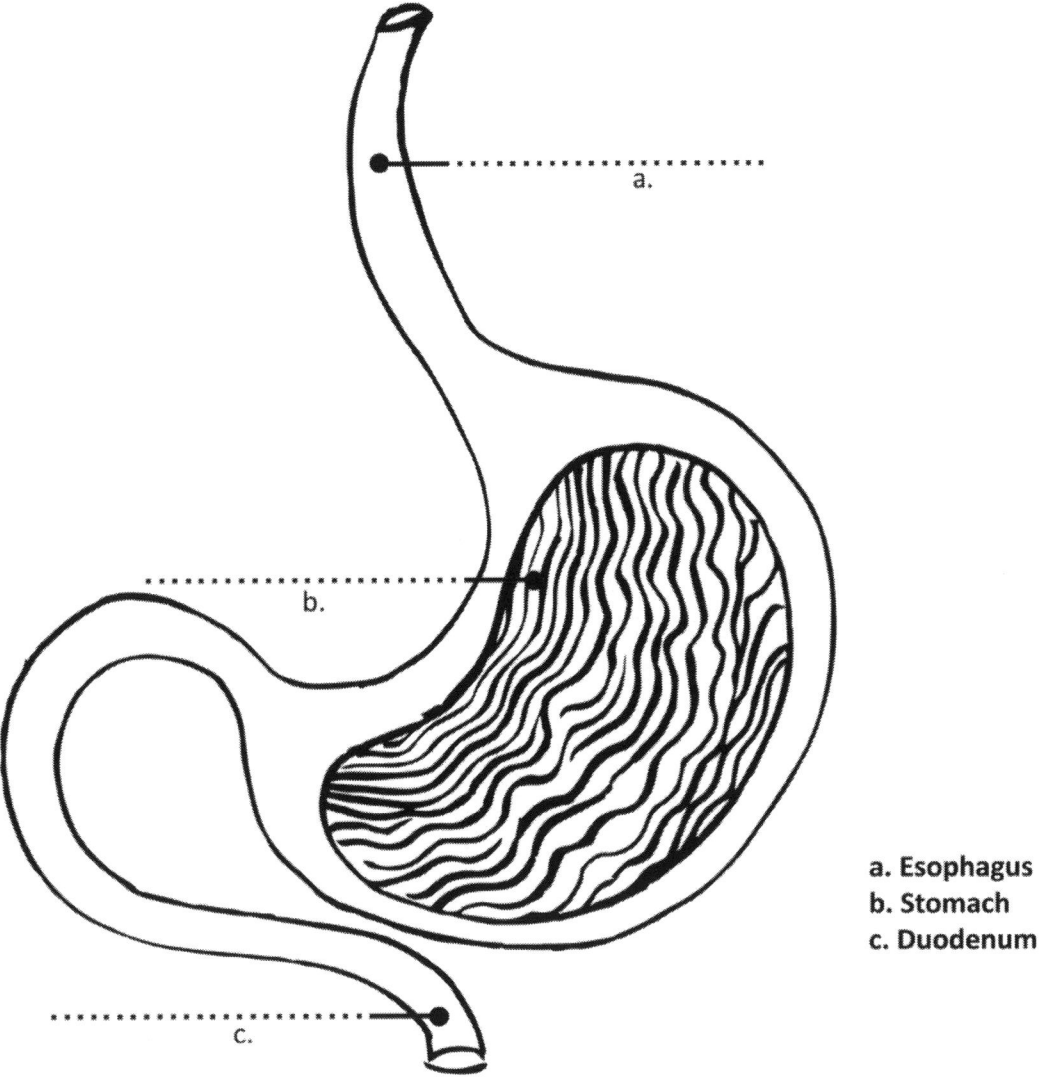

a. Esophagus
b. Stomach
c. Duodenum

Major Functions of the Stomach:
The main function of the stomach is to break down and digest food in order to extract necessary nutrients from what you have eaten.

How you can care for your Stomach:
Avoid eating late at night, Drink fluids after meals rather than during, Try to relax after meals.

THE TONGUE

Activity:
1. Find a coloring sample on the book covers.
2. Color the picture below and Fill in the Labelling.
3. Can you tell the major functions of the Tongue?
4. How can you take care of your Tongue?

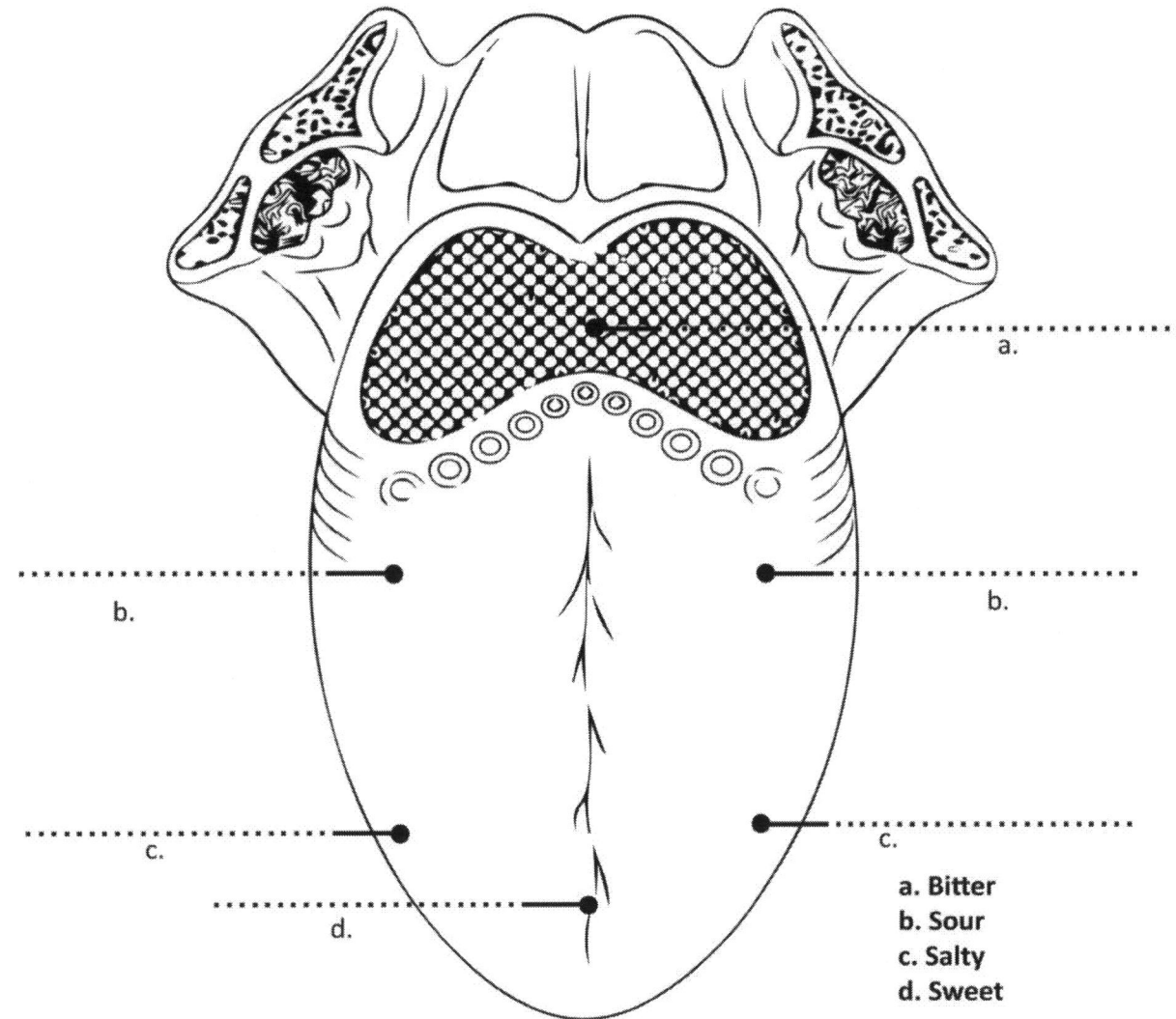

a. Bitter
b. Sour
c. Salty
d. Sweet

Major Functions of the Tongue:
The tongue facilitates the movement of food during mastication and assists swallowing. It is also used for speech and taste.

How you can care for your Tongue:
Clean your tongue once in the morning and once in the evening before bedtime with a tongue cleaner.

THE KIDNEY

Activity:
1. Find a coloring sample on the book covers.
2. Color the picture below and Fill in the Labelling.
3. Can you tell the major functions of the Kidney?
4. How can you take care of your Kidney?

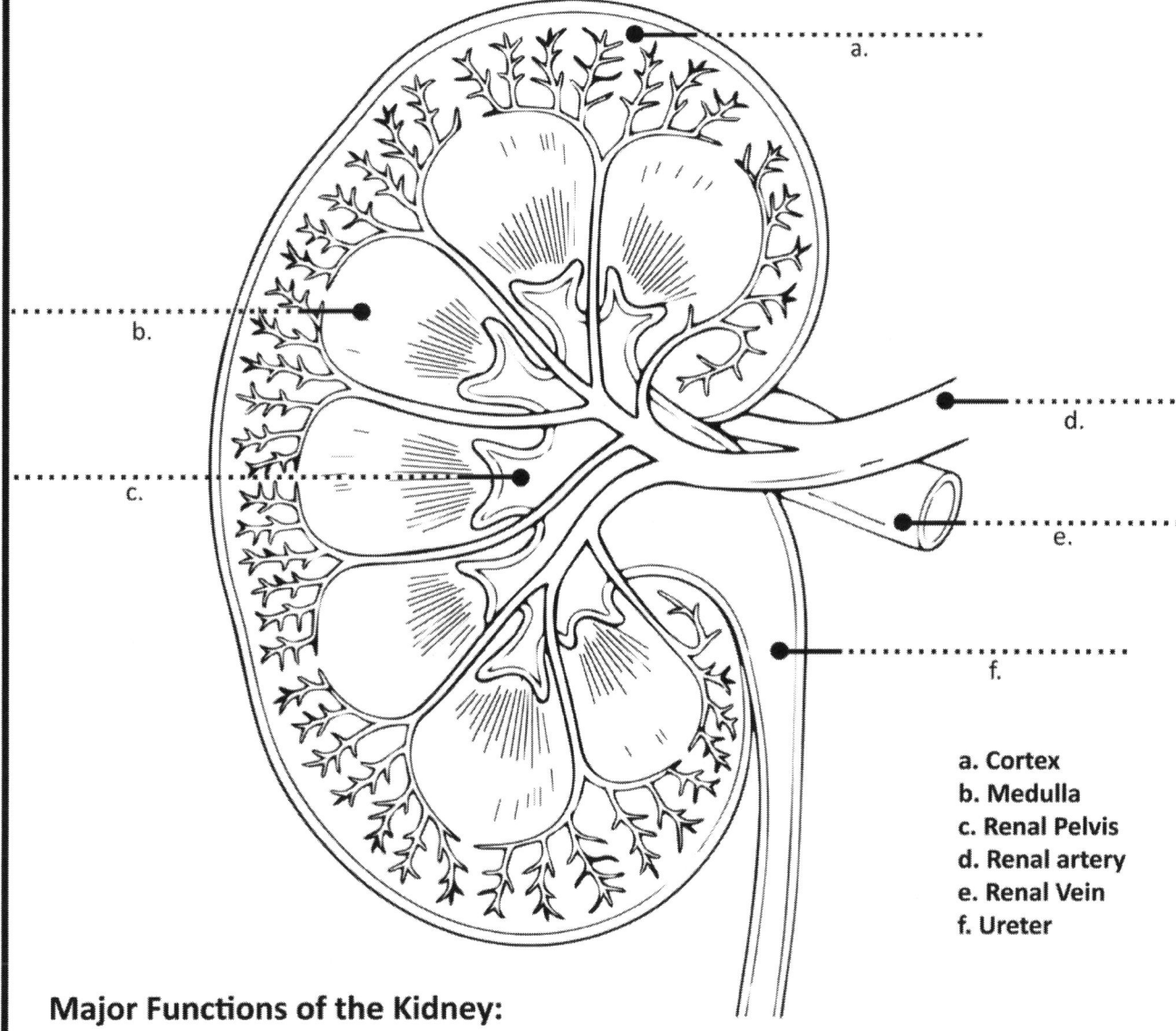

a. Cortex
b. Medulla
c. Renal Pelvis
d. Renal artery
e. Renal Vein
f. Ureter

Major Functions of the Kidney:
The kidney performs different functions such as removing waste products from the blood and regulating the water fluid levels in the body.

How you can care for your Kidney:
Eat healthy foods, Exercise regularly, keep your body Hydrated, avoid smoking.

THE LIVER

Activity:
1. Find a coloring sample on the book covers.
2. Color the picture below and Fill in the Labelling.
3. Can you tell the major functions of the Liver?
4. How can you take care of your Liver?

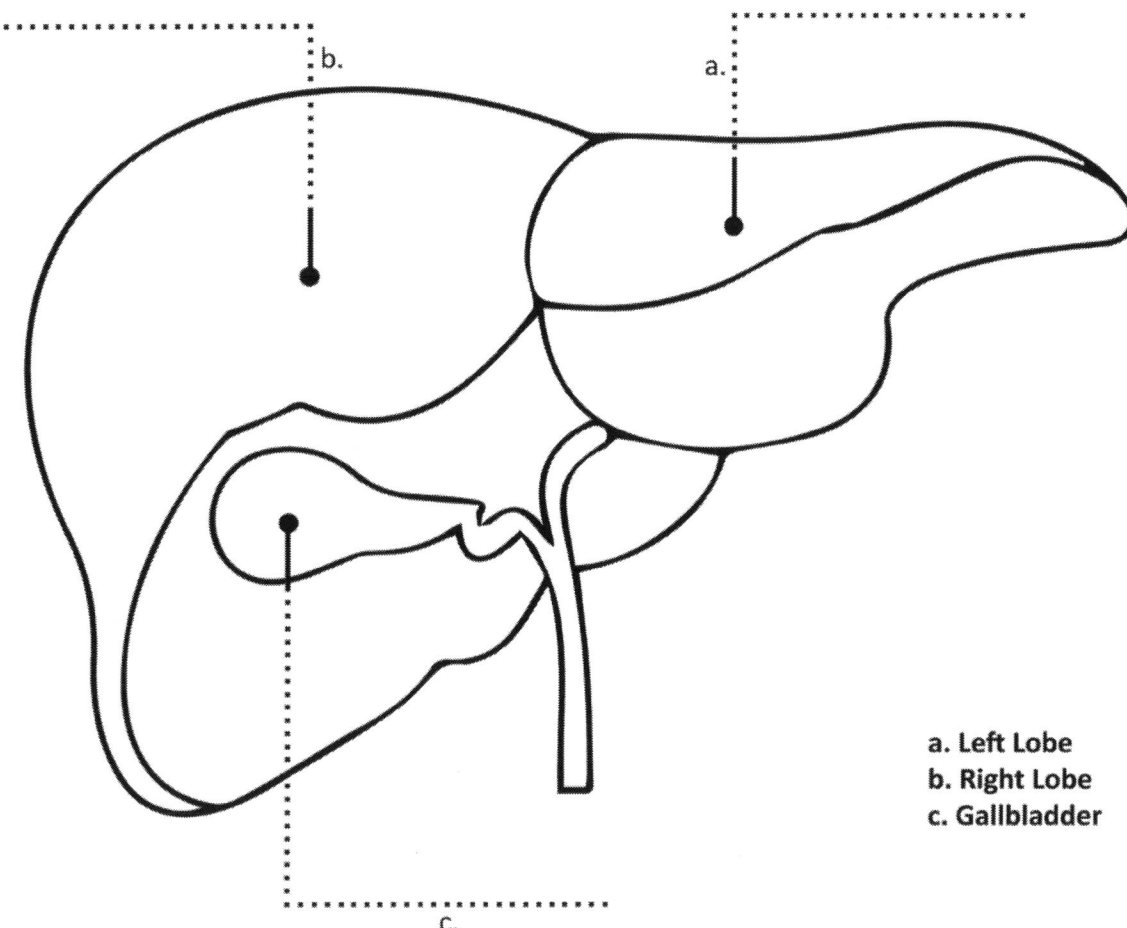

a. Left Lobe
b. Right Lobe
c. Gallbladder

Major Functions of the Liver:
The liver's main job is to filter the blood coming from the digestive tract, before passing it to the rest of the body.

How you can care for your Liver:
Eat a healthy diet and get regular exercise, avoid alcohol abuse.

THE LUNGS

Activity:
1. Find a coloring sample on the book covers.
2. Color the picture below and Fill in the Labelling.
3. Can you tell the major functions of the Lungs?
4. How can you take care of your Lungs?

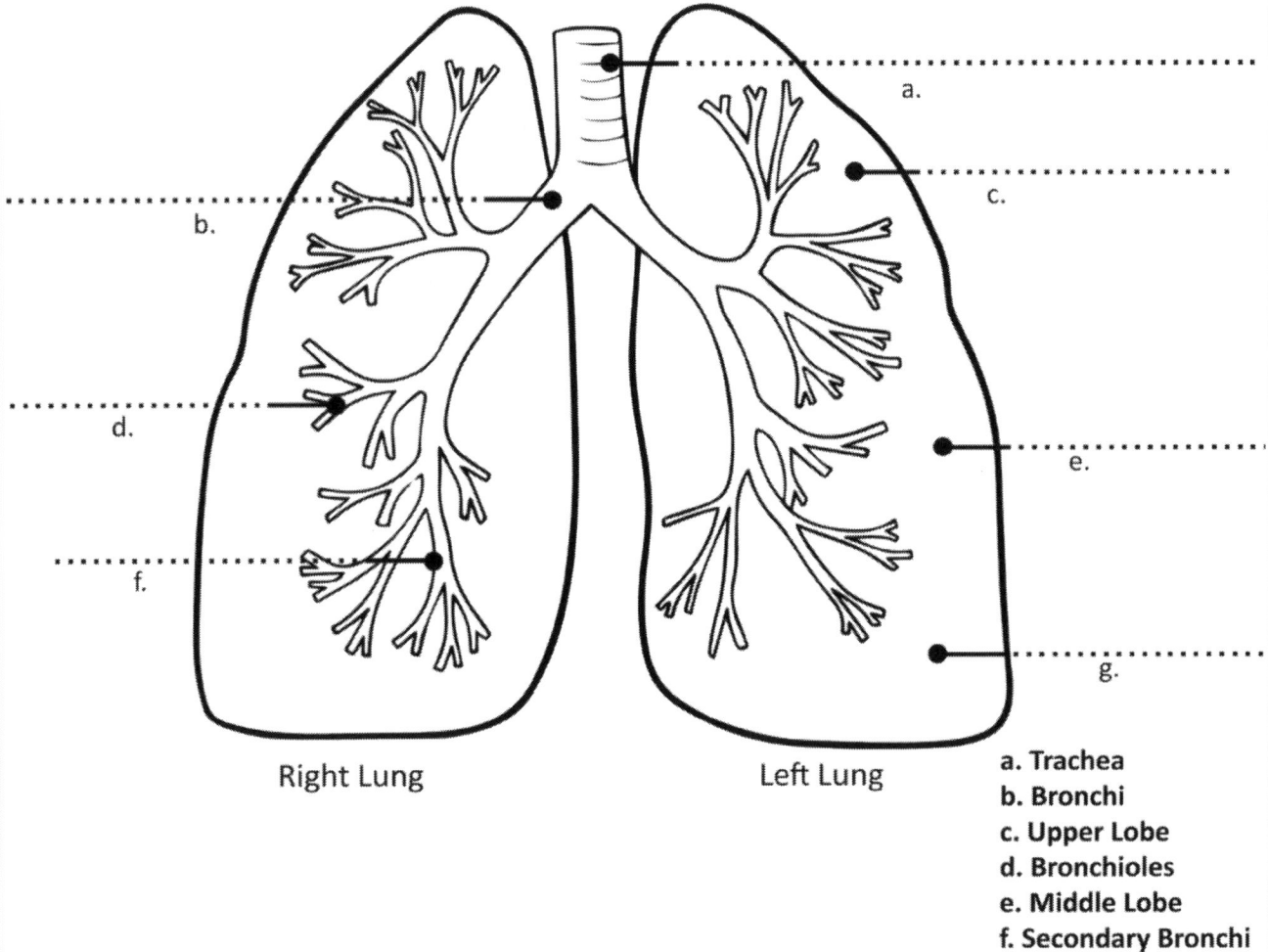

Right Lung   Left Lung

a. Trachea
b. Bronchi
c. Upper Lobe
d. Bronchioles
e. Middle Lobe
f. Secondary Bronchi
g. Lower Lobe

Major Functions of the Lungs:
The main function of the lungs is extracting oxygen from inhaled air for distribution via the bloodstream to every cell in the body.

How you can care for your Lungs:
Drink lots of water, avoid smoking, stay away from polluted air, engage in regular Aerobic exercises.

THE HAND BONES

Activity:
1. Find a coloring sample on the book covers.
2. Color the picture below and Fill in the Labelling.
3. Can you tell the major functions of the Hand Bones?
4. How can you take care of your Hand bonest?

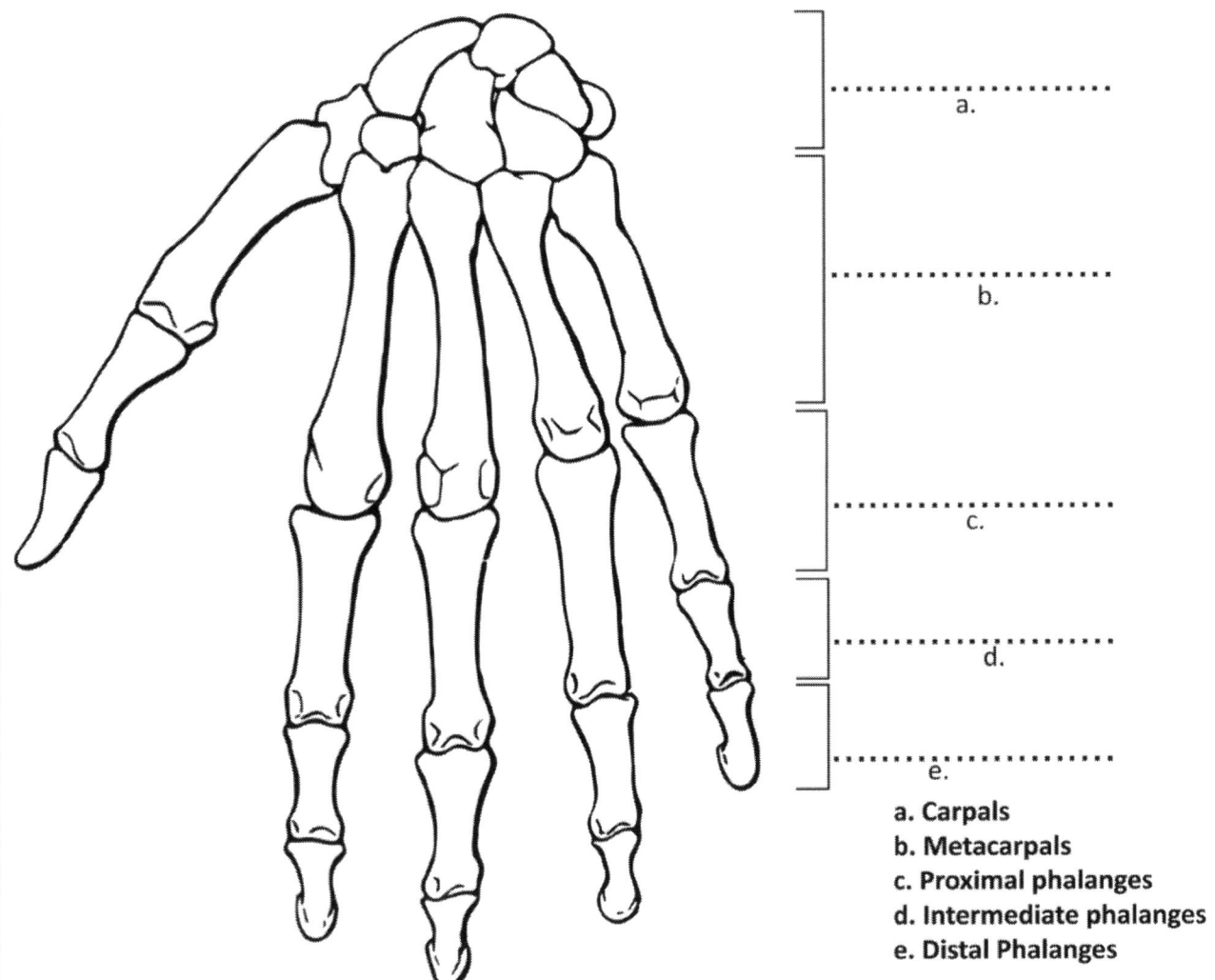

a. Carpals
b. Metacarpals
c. Proximal phalanges
d. Intermediate phalanges
e. Distal Phalanges

Major Functions of the Hand bones:
The hand bones support the hand to carry out its many functions such as; writing, holding, carrying, playing games, using a computer, texting on phones.

How you can care for your Hand bones:
Get enough vitamin D to keep your bones strong Vitamin D helps you absorb calcium in foods. You can find vitamin D in: Milk, Margarine, Egg yolks, Fatty fish like salmon and sardines.

THE LARGE INTESTINE

Activity:
1. Find a coloring sample on the book covers.
2. Color the picture below and Fill in the Labelling.
3. Can you tell the major functions of the Large Intestine?
4. How can you take care of your Large Intestine?

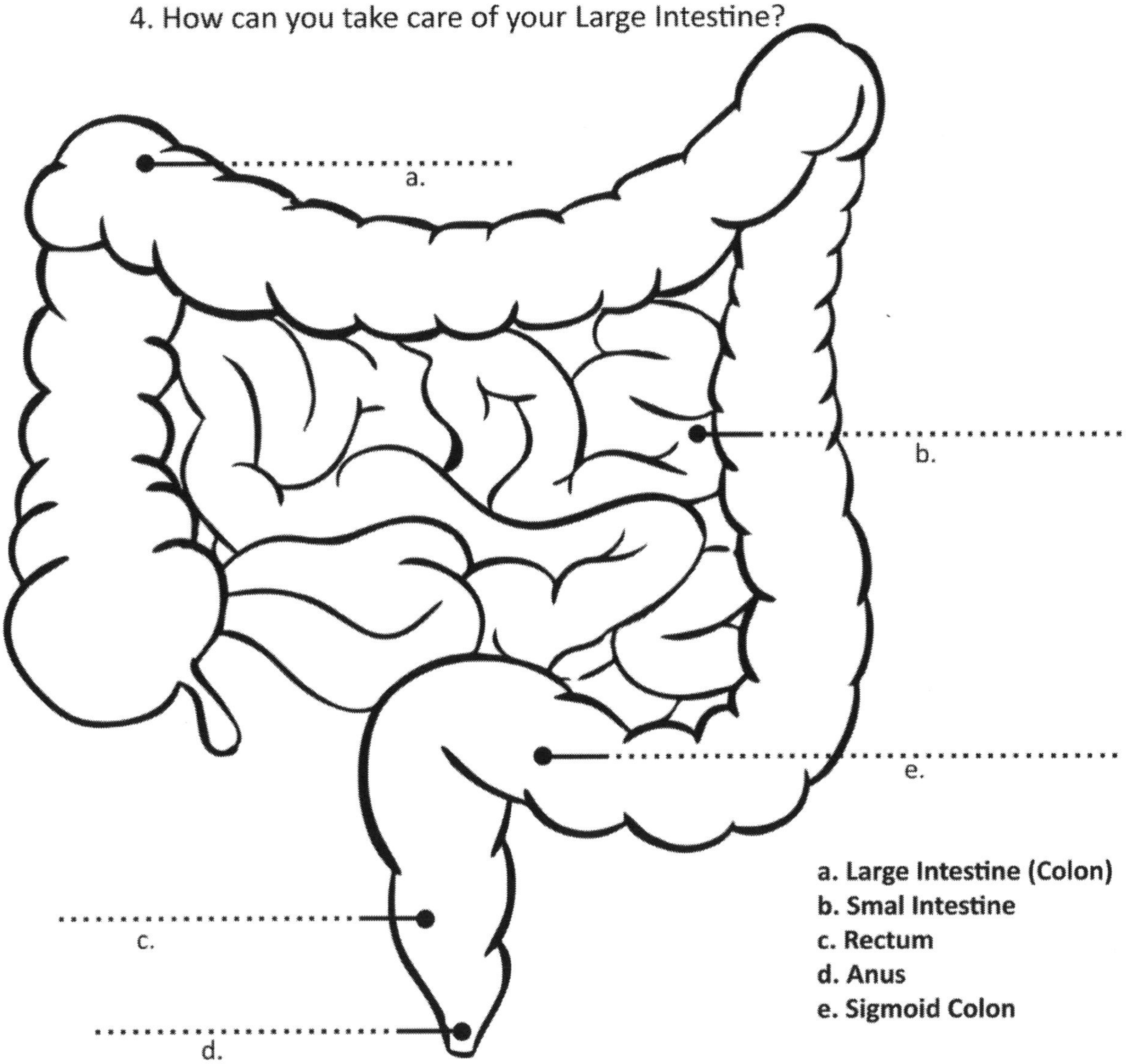

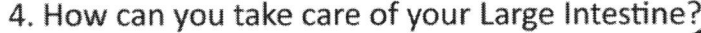

a.
b.
c.
e.
d.

a. Large Intestine (Colon)
b. Smal Intestine
c. Rectum
d. Anus
e. Sigmoid Colon

Major Functions of the Large Intestine:
The major function of the large intestine is to absorb water from the remaining indigestible food matter and transmit the useless waste material to the anus to be discharged from the body.

How you can care for your Large Intestine:
Eat a high-fiber diet, Limit foods that are high in fat, Stay hydrated, Exercise regularly.

THE SKULL (SIDE VIEW)

Activity:
1. Find a coloring sample on the book covers.
2. Color the picture below and Fill in the Labelling.
3. Can you tell the major functions of the Skull?
4. How can you take care of your Skull?

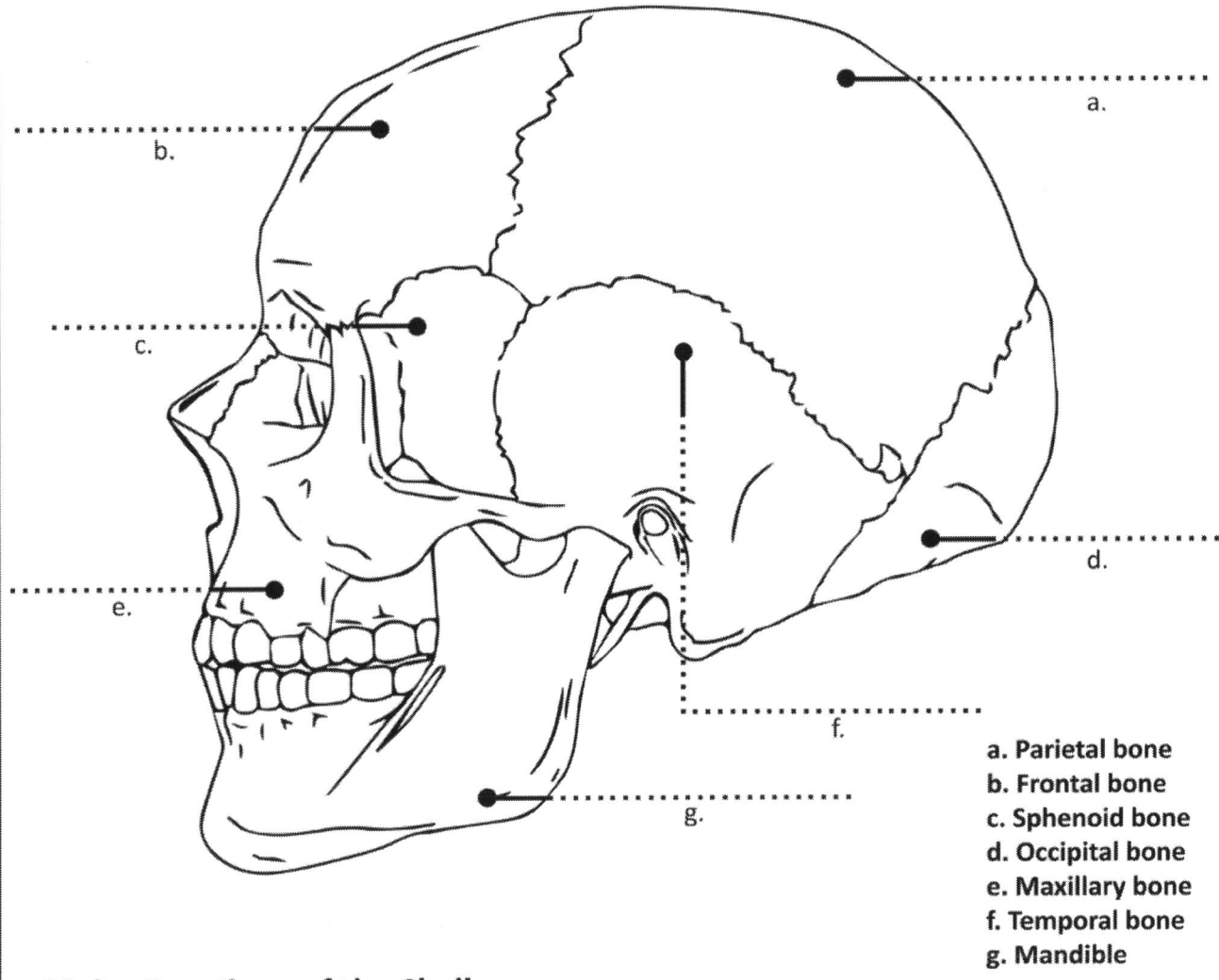

a. Parietal bone
b. Frontal bone
c. Sphenoid bone
d. Occipital bone
e. Maxillary bone
f. Temporal bone
g. Mandible

Major Functions of the Skull:
It supports the structures of the face and provides a protective cavity for the brain.

How you can care for your Skull:
Get enough vitamin D to keep your bones strong, Vitamin D helps you absorb calcium in foods. You can find vitamin D in: Milk, Margarine, Egg yolks, Fatty fish like salmon and sardines.

THE TOOTH

Activity:
1. Find a coloring sample on the book covers.
2. Color the picture below and Fill in the Labelling.
3. Can you tell the major functions of the Tooth?
4. How can you take care of your Tooth?

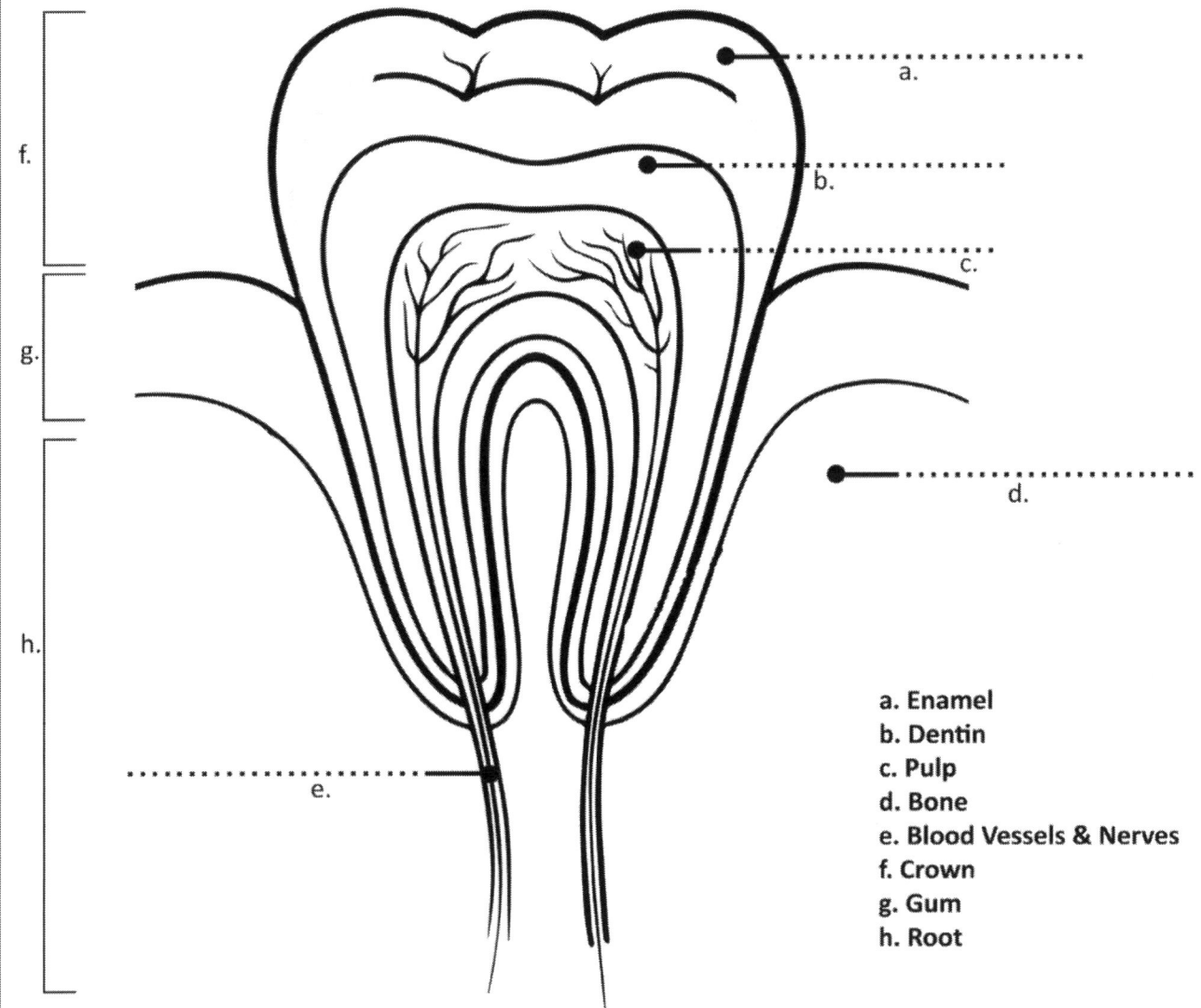

a. Enamel
b. Dentin
c. Pulp
d. Bone
e. Blood Vessels & Nerves
f. Crown
g. Gum
h. Root

Major Functions of the Tooth:
Your tooth helps you chew food, which makes the food easier to digest.

How you can care for your Tooth:
Brush your teeth twice a day with fluoride toothpaste, Floss once a day, Cut down on sugary foods and drinks, avoid smoking, Visit your dentist regularly, Eat a well-balanced diet.

Manufactured by Amazon.ca
Bolton, ON